In Pen's tent

In Pen's tent is Jack's cat.

Jack's fat cat
in a big hat!

In Pen's tent is Dad's pig.

Dad's big pig
in a big wig!

In Pen's tent is Mum's pug.

Mum's pug
has a jug and a mug.

In Pen's tent is the red fox.

The red fox
is in his box!

In Pen's tent is Rob's frog.

Rob's frog
jumps off the log!

In Pen's tent is Pen's Gran.

Pen's Gran has a big fan!

In Pen's tent is ...

Pen,
just Pen.